This book belongs to

COLOR TEST PAGE

COLOR TEST PAGE

TRICK OR TREAT

31
OCTOBER

LET'S
PARTY

TRICK OR TREAT

HAPPY
HALLOWEEN

YUM

31
OCTOBER

TRICK
OR
TREAT

HAPPY
HALLOWEEN

31
OCTOBER

HAPPY HALLOWEEN

31
OCTOBER

NIGHT

SPOKY

LET'S
PARTY

HAPPY HALLOWEEN

CPSIA information can be obtained
at www.ICGtesting.com
Printed in the USA
LVHW101059211019
634832LV00007B/2577/P

9 781699 306284